X-treme DISASTERS
THAT CHANGED AMERICA

TORNADO!
The 1974 Super Outbreak

by Jacqueline A. Ball

Consultant: Daniel H. Franck, Ph.D.

BEARPORT
PUBLISHING COMPANY, INC.

New York, New York

Credits

Front Cover, inset, Associated Press / AP; background, AP Photo / Great Bend Tribune, Patrick Richardson.

Back Cover, tornado, National Weather Service Forecast Office Wilmington Ohio; Map, NOAA.

Title page, Associated Press / AP; Page 4-5, National Weather Service Forecast Office Wilmington Ohio; 6, Associated Press / AP; 7, Bettmann / CORBIS; 9, National Weather Service Forecast Office Wilmington Ohio; 10, Louis Pappas and Monica Ponomarev, 11, David Hies / CORBIS SYGMA; 12-13, Associated Press / AP; 14-15, Howard Bluestein / Photo Researchers, Inc.; 16-17, AP Photo/J. Pat Carter; 18-19, Jim Reed / Science Photo Library / Photo Researchers, Inc.; 19, inset, Warren Faidley / Weatherstock.com; 20, Jim Reed / Photo Researchers, Inc.; 21, AP Photo/Great Bend Tribune, Patrick Richardson; 22-23, Jim Reed / CORBIS; 24, Associated Press / AP; 25, Larry Mulvehill / The Image Works; 26, Greene County Public Library, Xenia, Ohio; 27, Andy Woodruff; 29, AP Photo / The Daily Oklahoman, Paul Hellstern.

Design and production by Dawn Beard Creative, Triesta Hall of Blu-Design, and Octavo Design and Production, Inc.

Library of Congress Cataloging-in-Publication Data

Ball, Jacqueline A.
  Tornado! : the 1974 super outbreak / by Jacqueline A. Ball ; consultant, Daniel H. Franck.
      p. cm. — (X-treme disasters that changed America)
  Includes bibliographical references and index.
  ISBN 1-59716-009-1 (lib. bdg.)—ISBN 1-59716-032-6 (pbk.)
1. Tornadoes—Ohio—Xenia—Juvenile literature. 2. Tornadoes—United States—Juvenile literature.
3. Tornado warning systems—United States—Juvenile literature. I. Title. II. Series.

QC955.2.B35 2005
551.55'3—dc22

                              2004020744

For more information, write to Bearport Publishing Company, Inc., 101 Fifth Avenue, Suite 6R, New York, New York 10003. Printed in the United States of America.

1 2 3 4 5 6 7 8 9 10

Table of Contents

It's a Tornado!

Catherine Wilson was nine years old. She lived in a town called Xenia (ZEEN-yuh), Ohio. It was almost time for supper on April 3, 1974.

For people in Xenia, supper would have to wait. Something strange was happening outside.

The sky was purple. A large cloud hung down low. It was wide on top and narrow on the bottom. The cloud touched the ground. Now it was spinning through Catherine's town!

There was a roar like a plane taking off. Then **hail** hit the windows. A **tornado** had just struck.

◀ Xenia, Ohio—April 3, 1974

Most tornadoes occur between 3 p.m. and 9 p.m.

A Town Torn Apart

A tornado is a powerful storm. It has strong, circling winds. A weak tornado can break branches off trees. A strong tornado can lift up anything in its way. A tornado can take a roof off of a house and turn over a truck.

Hail and lightning often come with a tornado. They can cause as much damage as the winds. The tornado in Xenia killed 33 people. More than a thousand were hurt. It knocked down hundreds of buildings, including the high school. Luckily, school was out for the day. In only nine minutes, the town was pulled apart.

The wind in the Xenia tornado was very strong. It reached speeds of more than 200 miles per hour. A car can travel on a highway at about 65 miles per hour.

A Super Outbreak

    Xenia's giant tornado was part of a group of 148 tornadoes. A group of tornadoes is an **outbreak**. An even larger group is called a super outbreak. The tornado that hit Xenia was part of a super outbreak that went through 13 states and parts of Canada. The tornadoes cut a path almost 2,500 miles long.

The "red" states were the ones hit by the tornadoes.

The Super Outbreak of 1974 lasted 16 hours. It finally ended on April 4. More than 5,000 people were hurt and about 315 people were dead. Some people had died of **heart attacks**. The tornadoes had scared them to death.

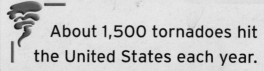
About 1,500 tornadoes hit the United States each year.

How Does a Tornado Form?

Tornadoes begin in **thunderclouds**. Winds high in the cloud blow faster than winds lower down. Sometimes high and low winds blow in different directions. The air starts to spin. Power builds up at the cloud's center. The bottom of the cloud often stretches to a point. Now the cloud looks like a **funnel**. When the cloud touches the ground, it's a tornado.

A Tornado Is Born

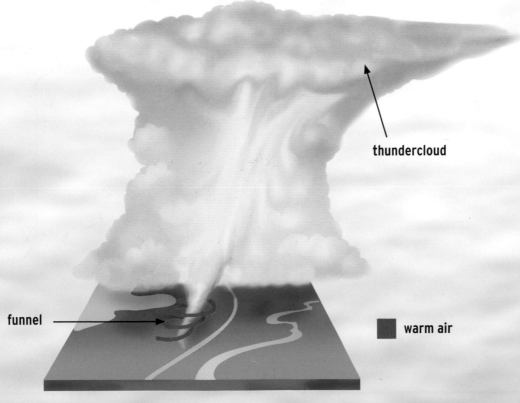

thundercloud

funnel

warm air

Tornadoes get their energy from thunderstorms. When this energy reaches the ground during a tornado, it's in the form of powerful winds that circle the tornado's funnel.

A tornado's color comes from the dirt and waste it carries. The Xenia tornado was full of pieces of something black. Some people thought those pieces were blackbirds. They were really tiles, lifted off the roofs of houses.

▲ This tornado picked up a lot of dirt and waste as it swept through Salt Lake City, Utah in 1999.

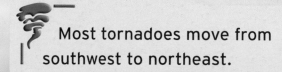
Most tornadoes move from southwest to northeast.

The F Scale

Some tornadoes have more power than others. Scientists measure a tornado's power with the Fujita (foo-JEE-tuh) Scale. Theodore Fujita came up with this scale. It's also called the F Scale.

The Fujita Scale

F Scale	Wind Speed	Damage
F0	40-72 mph	Branches break off trees; light damage
F1	73-112 mph	Mobile homes fall over; moving cars pushed off road
F2	113-157 mph	Roofs torn off buildings; trees uprooted
F3	158-206 mph	Trains knocked over; walls of houses torn off
F4	207-260 mph	Large structures and cars thrown long distances
F5	261-318 mph	Sturdy houses lifted off foundations; steel and concrete structures damaged; bark ripped off trees

Every tornado is given a number on the F Scale. The number depends on a tornado's wind speed and the **damage** it can cause. Number F0 is the weakest tornado. Number F5 is the strongest. The Super Outbreak of 1974 had tornadoes reaching from F1 to F5. The one that hit Xenia was an F5.

▼ These homes were destroyed after an F4 tornado hit Oklahoma in 1999.

About one F5 tornado occurs in the United States every year. In the Super Outbreak of 1974 there were seven.

Could a Tornado Hit Your Town?

The answer is yes. Tornadoes can strike at any time. In the United States, however, most tornadoes occur in April and May. Texas, Oklahoma, and Kansas are the states with the most tornadoes.

These states are part of a larger area called Tornado Alley, which reaches from Texas to Nebraska. Above Tornado Alley, cold dry winds from Canada often hit warm, wet winds from the Gulf of Mexico. When cold and warm air run into each other, wild storms can occur.

◀ A 1999 tornado, one hour before it hit Oklahoma City, Oklahoma.

Tornadoes travel fastest over smooth, flat land.

More Tornadoes, Fewer Deaths

No tornado outbreak since 1974 has been as large. However, on June 7, 1984, a group of 45 tornadoes hit Iowa, Minnesota, and Wisconsin. In one town, only the water tower was left standing. On May 3, 1999, 74 tornadoes cut through Oklahoma and Kansas. One of them hit Oklahoma City and caused a billion dollars worth of damage.

The number of tornadoes each year seems to be growing. The number of people killed in each tornado, however, is going down. Scientists are learning more about tornadoes all the time. What they learn is helping to keep us safer.

◀ A motorist tries to outrun a tornado in Oklahoma.

The deadliest tornado in the United States was the outbreak of March 18, 1925. It killed 689 people in Missouri, Illinois, and Indiana.

New Tools for Tracking

Today scientists have powerful instruments to track tornadoes. They use a special tool called Doppler **radar**. This radar searches the sky for signs of tornadoes and other bad weather. Then it sends signals to weather stations. It sends new signals every six minutes.

▶ The National Weather Service office in Dodge City, Kansas

A tornado "watch" means a tornado might happen. A tornado "warning" is more serious. It means a tornado has been seen.

Now weather scientists know a storm is coming when it's hundreds of miles away. They can find where it may strike. They can tell if it's going to turn into a tornado. Then they can warn people. These warnings have saved many lives since the Super Outbreak of 1974.

▼ In this Doppler radar image, the hook near the lower left corner means that a tornado may form.

Looking for Trouble

Some people want to see tornadoes up close. These people are called **storm chasers**. Storm chasers sometimes drive hundreds of miles to reach a storm. Hail may hit their trucks while lightning flashes down at them. Wind may blow rain from every direction. Still, storm chasers drive on.

◀ Storm chasers prepare to chase a storm.

Most storm chasers in the United States travel around Tornado Alley. Many of them, however, spend most of their time hunting for the tornadoes rather than seeing them.

◄ A tornado spins to the ground in Kansas.

Some storm chasers are weather scientists. Others are just people curious about these storms.

Doppler on Wheels

Now storm chasers can get into the path of a tornado with the help of Doppler on Wheels (DOW). DOW is made up of a group of trucks. Each truck has a Doppler radar unit on its roof.

These machines help scientists gather more information with fewer mistakes than regular Doppler radar. They also help storm chasers map tornadoes. These facts help scientists understand how tornadoes form and grow.

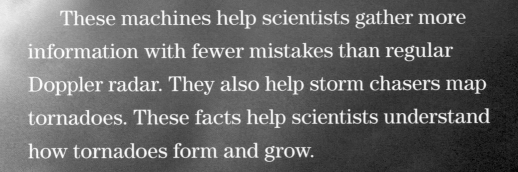

There is a new machine called rapid-scan DOW. It's even faster than DOW and can gather more kinds of information.

Warnings that Work

In the 1970s, there were 100 weather radio stations. Now there are 900. They announce storm warnings all the time. Radio warnings are important. Often there is no electricity during a storm, so TVs don't work. Many radios, however, run on batteries.

▲ An outdoor weather siren in Oklahoma City, Oklahoma

In Xenia, there are now ten warning **sirens**. They will go off 12 minutes before a tornado is supposed to hit. Every one in Xenia knows what to do if the siren sounds. They run inside their homes. They stay in the center of a ground floor room, such as a basement. They keep away from windows.

▼ A National Weather Service scientist reads the forecast.

Don't stay in a mobile home during a tornado warning. Instead, find the closest brick or wooden building. Wait out the storm there.

A Town Back Together

Catherine Wilson and her mom stayed in the bathroom. They weren't hurt. Their roof had a big hole in it. Other houses blew off their bases. Xenia now has new building rules because of the tornado. Roofs are made stronger so they don't easily lift off. Walls are built better to handle higher winds.

◀ An aerial view of Xenia after the tornado hit

In Xenia, some houses now have "safe rooms." These rooms are made of steel and brick. They should stay standing even if the houses blow away. A super tornado outbreak could happen again. If it does, more people will live to tell about it.

▲ Xenia today

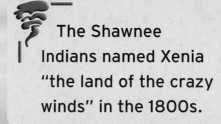

The Shawnee Indians named Xenia "the land of the crazy winds" in the 1800s.

Just the Facts

The Super Outbreak of 1974

- In Xenia, the wind was so strong it blew bits of dirt through clothing. The dirt stuck in people's skin.
- Of the 148 tornadoes in the Super Outbreak, 118 had paths over a mile long.
- It took 200 trucks three months to take away all the waste left in Xenia after the tornado.

Strange Things Tornadoes Do

- Tornadoes have lifted frogs out of ponds and dropped them miles away. People have thought it was "raining frogs."
- In 1917, a tornado carried a jar of pickles 25 miles. It dropped the jar without breaking it.
- In 1955, an F5 tornado hit Udall, Kansas. It destroyed half the town. It also pulled a man named Fred Dye out of his house and out of his shoes and then dumped him into a tree. He was not hurt.

Improvements Because of the Super Outbreak of 1974

- More radio weather stations
- More warning sirens
- Stronger and safer buildings
- Better school safety plans

▲ In Oklahoma, a tornado is about to touch ground in 1998. This tornado toppled a radio tower and turned over some cars and trucks.

Glossary

damage (DAM-ij)   harm; ruin

funnel (FUHN-uhl)   an open cone with a tube at the end, used for pouring something into a container

hail (HAYL)   small balls of ice that sometimes fall from the clouds during thunderstorms

heart attacks (HART-uh-TAKS)   sudden instances of chest pain that occur when a person's heart is not pumping blood properly

outbreak (OUT-*brake*)   a sudden start of something

radar (RAY-dar)   a measuring instrument in which radio waves are used to locate distant objects

sirens (SYE-ruhnz)   pieces of equipment that make a loud, shrill sound to warn people of danger

storm chasers (STORM CHAYS-urz)   people who chase tornadoes to see them up close

thunderclouds (THUHN-dur-*klouds*)   large, dark clouds that produce thunder and lightning

tornado (tor-NAY-doh)   a violent, whirling column of air that looks like a dark, cone-shaped cloud that moves quickly over the land

Bibliography

Blumenthal, Ralph. "Hot on the Trail of Tornadoes: Where Too Close Is Just Right." *New York Times*. June 7, 2004.

Cerveny, Randy, and Joseph T. Schaefer. "Tornado Oddities." *Weatherwise*. July/August 2002.

Miller, Peter. "Tornado!" *National Geographic Society*. 1999.

Moores, Lew. "1974 Tornado Tore Xenia's Heart." *Cincinnati Enquirer*. March 30, 1999.

Osborne, Will, and Mary Pope Osborne. *Twisters and Other Terrible Storms: A Nonfiction Companion to <u>Twister on Tuesday</u> (Magic Tree House Research Guide)*. New York, NY: Random House Children's Books (2003).

Sharp, Debra. "Super Tornado Outbreak." *USA Today*. April 2, 1999.

Read More

Berger, Melvin, and Gilda Berger. *Do Tornadoes Really Twist? Questions and Answers About Tornadoes.* New York, NY: Scholastic (2000).

Simon, Seymour. *Tornadoes.* New York, NY: HarperCollins (1999).

Learn More Online

Visit this Web site to learn more about tornadoes:
- http://www.ucar.edu/educ_outreach/webweather/xenia.html

Index

About the Author

Jacqueline A. Ball has written and produced more than one hundred books for kids and adults. She lives in New York City and Old Lyme, Connecticut.